Honey Lavender Publishing

Copyright 2021 Cheryl Palladino and Rachael Ostrowski
www.honeylavenderpublishing.com
All rights reserved.

Printed in the United States of America
ISBN-978-0-578-98751-4

No part of this publication may be reproduced, stored, distributed, or transmitted in any form or by any means, including photocopying, recording, or other electronic or mechanical methods, without the prior written permission of the publisher, except in the case of brief quotations embodied in critical reviews and certain other non commercial uses permitted by copyright law.

Summary: Addie was looking forward to spending the year with her best friend Jozetta. Thank goodness she had her Me-Cave to navigate the unexpected change.

Join Addie as she takes an underwater adventure to explore how to become a more flexible thinker. Along the way she meets some new friends who help her to accept things that are out of her control and see the good there is with the new plan. A perfect story for teachers and parents to foster conversations about change, especially when it is unexpected!

(1.Inclusion 2.Calm 3.feelings 4.anger management 5.emotions 6.behavior 7.social emotional 8.self-awareness 9.self-management 10.social awareness 11.relationship management 12.responsible decision- making)

honey Lavender Publishing

ADDIE'S ME-CAVE
SEASIDE FRIENDS

written by:
Rachael Ostrowski and **Cheryl Palladino**

illustrated by:
Naidielee Laquindanum

Dear Loving Adult,

This story introduces the importance of "flexible thinking" as kids navigate the many changes of childhood. Life is not always smooth sailing, and when the waves come rolling in, coping skills can help us be more prepared to ride them. Children are oftentimes presented with change that is out of their control, and this can result in feelings of frustration and helplessness. Teaching and modeling skills, such as deep breathing, asking questions, using their smarts, and being flexible, helps children build their social-emotional toolbox.

At the end of the story, we have included a visual aid to help children remember ways to be flexible and cope with changes. Other ways you can support children in learning these skills are to play games and do other activities that model flexible thinking. Also, if you witness them using flexible thinking, make sure to acknowledge their efforts.

We hope you enjoy the story and see this book as a great addition to your social-emotional support library.

Sincerely,
Cheryl + Rachael

To all the class pets.
Thank you for teaching our children awareness, kindness, and compassion.

It was hot and Addie felt like she was a dripping ice cream cone.

She had just finished playing sharks and minnows in the sprinklers outside, and she was soaked.

Summer was coming to an end and school was about to begin.

I am so excited to see my friends again! she thought.
She would get to see her best friend Jozetta, after three month's at home.
She and Jozetta were going to be in the same class this year!

ADDIE!

"Addie," called her mom. "I have something important to share with you."

Addie smiled big. It was time for back-to-school shopping. She loved picking out new colorful notebooks, folders, pens, and a backpack.

I'm getting the blue bag with the shark on the front, she thought out loud.

Addie wrapped herself in a towel and ran inside. She grabbed her supply list hanging on the refrigerator and plopped down on the blue fluffy couch next to her mom.

This must be how it feels to sit on a squishy jellyfish, she thought.

Then, with a loud cry, Addie blurted out,

"IT'S NOT FAIR!"

Addie jumped off the couch and headed straight to her special cave. Her mom had made her the space to use when her thoughts started getting too big. The cave would help her work through all of these feelings she was having after hearing such terrible news about school. Addie felt her tummy churning like she was riding on a big wave in the deep blue sea.

She felt a little sad, a little angry, and even a little annoyed. Addie turned the sign on the front of her cupboard door to read, *I need alone time.* She abrupty changed the feelings wheel to point to *mad*. Then she slammed the cupboard door behind her and gave her trusted penguin, Puffy, a tight squeeze.

With Puffy snuggled by her side, Addie studied her breathing card and took five slow, deep breaths. She closed her eyes and felt the rushing waves in her tummy turn into a calm, gentle tide. The thumping in her heart started to slow. She opened her eyes and looked in her kaleidoscope.

Addie and Puffy were wearing scuba suits, masks, flippers and floating in the middle of a bunch of colorful fish. Addie looked around and saw Puffy jumping on a jellyfish trampoline.

"Wee-wee-wee," Puffy squealed.

Addie excitedly thought, This must be what an underwater playground looks like!

All the fish were giggling and playing games.

An optus was swinging on some kelp bars, an eel was playing in the sand, and some crabs were sliding down a bumpy coral slide.

Swimming next to Addie was a golden yellow fish. He had a long body, a blunt face, a forked tail fin, and a long dorsal fin.

"Hola. My name is Durado, and this is my first day here at my new school. I moved here from South America, and I do not have any friends. I miss my old school and the way we used to do things."

Addie understood how he felt.

"I've never been here before, either. My name is Addie, and this is my penguin, Puffy."

Just then, a large octopus wearing a headband and glasses blew the whistle from around her neck in three long, loud blows.

"Today is our first day of sea-school, and we will play a new game. Let's all make a circle."

The sea animals gathered in a circle except for Durado. He had snuck away to hide behind a large bunch of algae.

Addie followed Dorado to his hiding spot.

"A new game sounds like fun. Why did you swim away?"

Dorado looked down with sad eyes. "Trying new things makes me feel scared. I only know how to play the games from my last school. Mis amigos and my favorite coral slide are at my old school. I don't want things to change. No es justo!"

"I know how you feel. My school will be different this year, too. I won't get to be in my classroom or play with my friends. I will have to learn on a computer."

Dorado looked surprised. "That sounds fun! I love working on computers! There are so many fun games and activities to do, and you can choose where you do your school work. You can even talk to your friends and family using the computer and feel like they are with you."

Durado stopped and looked at Addie. He had an idea.

"Even though my family moves every time the seasons change, I can still talk to mis amigos y mi familia on the computer."

Addie was intrigued. "I didn't think about the good parts of learning at home."

Addie thought about how she could still see Jozetta on the computer every day and even get to sit at her fancy teal desk in her bedroom.

Dorado started to look less sad, so Addie continued, "Trying something new can feel uncomfortable at first, but it's how we grow and learn. I always feel proud of myself after I try!"

Addie pointed towards the fish playing a game with their teacher. "Do you want to try out the new playground and test the slippery coral slide? That one has a loopy-loop. I bet it is pretty speedy, and look! Zebra fish needs a slide partner."

Dorado did think the game looked fun. He slowly crept out of his hiding spot and swam over to the playground.

Addie watched as Durado joined Zebra to play. Addie could tell his nerves were floating away. It felt good to see Dorado making new friends and looking happy.

Addie yawned, "I think it's time to head home, Puffy."
Puffy was tired from all the fun playing with the underwater sea animals.

Addie heard the doorbell chime. She could hear faint familiar talking outside the cave. As she crawled out, her mom called her over to the front door. She was holding a bowl with a shimmering golden fish swimming inside. She set the bowl on the entryway table.

"Addie," said her mom, "I want to introduce you to your classroom pet. Your teacher dropped him off with a note. She said that classmates get to take turns caring for him, and because your name starts with A, you are first on the list!"

Addie felt happy bubbles in her tummy.

"I'm excited that this year will be different," Addie said to her mom as she approached the fish bowl. "I was scared of school being different at first, but after calming my body and thinking about it, I'm feeling better now."

Addie's mom smiled sweetly and put her arm around Addie.
"I'm glad to see that you are using flexible thinking. It is important to be open to new ideas when things are changing and our worries feel big."

Addie peered into the glass, taking a look at the golden fish. He was weaving in and out of a little plant at the bottom of the bowl.

Addie opened the note from her teacher. It read:

Meet Durado!

Dorado fish are found all over the globe. Ours is from Latin America. These fish are referred to as dorado, which means "golden." Dorado fish migrate when seasons change, and can be shy.

Please write about Durado's adventures each week. Tell us about all the new things he tried!

Sincerely,
Miss Eloise

Addie held Puffy up to take another look at the fish. As she leaned in, she closed one eye to examine the fish closer. To her surprise, Durado smiled and gave her a wink.

www.ingramcontent.com/pod-product-compliance
Lightning Source LLC
LaVergne TN
LVHW070124080526
838200LV00086B/332